# The Everything and The Nothing

# THE
# EVERYTHING
# AND THE
# NOTHING

———

MEHER BABA

SHERIAR
FOUNDATION

1995

# Introduction

These Discourses were given over the last two or three years to his disciples by one who needs no introduction because he is the Self of every self and has his home in every heart; but because we have forgotten this he has re-introduced himself to men as the Ancient One who is before all things were and will be after all things have ceased to exist.

In earlier times he was known as Jesus the Christ and Gotama the Buddha and Krishna the Lover and Rama the King. This time he is called Meher Baba. Later, after he has dropped his mortal body, men will probably add 'The Awakener' after his name, for he has said, I have come not to teach but to awaken.

Meher Baba asserts that he is God, Truth Absolute, and says he has taken form solely because of his compassion for suffering humanity. Man's suffering is great. Despite the propaganda programmes of 'things were never better' man's suffering is so great that he has devised the means of self-annihilation, to extinguish himself and his seed utterly. The question that now occupies the minds of all thinking men is how this destruction may be averted — for the power for this destruction is in the hands of men who are not morally equipped to be the custodians of such power.

This thinking is not in clear streams, but is rather as the cross-currents of an agitated sea seeking a channelled flow toward *Something* that can guarantee continued existence. With religionists this *Something* tends to take the form of *Someone*, the world Saviour which all religions promise.

Meher Baba says he *is* this *Something* or *Someone*.
'I am the One whom so many seek and so few find.'

Naturally many will not accept this assertion. Indeed,
while all men are praying for *Someone* or *Something*
to save the world, some will be praying that this Man
be saved from the gigantic deception of believing he is
God!

But Truth has never waited for us to accept It, but,
as the Wind listeth where It will, proclaims Itself
according to Its own sweet will and whim. It is as
natural for God-Man to assert, I am God, as it is for
us to assert, I am man. And it would be as laughable
for God-Man to say, I am not God, as it would be for
us to say, I am not man. Our ignorance of divine Truths
is colossal and our ideas about God are so elementary.

It takes some courage to accept God as God-Man,
for acceptance means surrender of one's individual ego-
life. However, since our cherished lives are no longer
ours but are in the hands of the first one who will give
an order for buttons to be pressed, surrender is not so
difficult!

But more courageous than those who surrender
themselves to God-Man would seem to be those, who,
expecting a *Someone* or a *Something,* remain true to
their *expectation* by denying the occurrence of the
Advent of God-Man *because they cannot prove he is
not* what he proclaims he is.

And perhaps more courageous than these are those
who continue to follow the westering false lights of
material progress while the beautiful silent Person of
God has already lit the east-sky with the Dawn of a
New Humanity. Presently the Sun of his Word will
break across the world, and his Glory will be manifest
to all.

Meanwhile the Discourses in this book — dictated

in silence by Meher Baba through hand-signs — may be said to be indications of the One Word of Truth that he will utter when he breaks his Silence and manifests his Godhood to men. *The Everything and The Nothing* constitutes a preparation of mind and heart to receive that One Word of Truth when he speaks it.

*Francis Brabazon*

1st November, 1962

# *Introduction to the New Edition*

Among the handful of books written by Meher Baba is this small gem. Though it contains only 113 pages of text, *The Everything and The Nothing* has so wide a range that it can keep one occupied heart and mind for many hours.

*The Everything and The Nothing* is full of fresh ideas. It has great sweetness, inspiration, and lyricism, all rooted in the clarity of true knowledge.

Gathered from messages given by Meher Baba in the late 1950s and early 1960s, *The Everything and The Nothing* is the best single source of the wisdom given by Meher Baba in his later years.

October 17, 1989          Ann Conlon
                          Myrtle Beach, South Carolina

# Contents

# 1

## *The Lover and the Beloved*

God is Love. And Love must love. And to love there must be a Beloved. But since God is Existence infinite and eternal there is no one for Him to love but Himself. And in order to love Himself He must imagine Himself as the Beloved whom He as the Lover imagines He loves.

Beloved and Lover implies separation. And separation creates longing; and longing causes search. And the wider and the more intense the search the greater the separation and the more terrible the longing.

When longing is most intense separation is complete, and the purpose of separation, which was that Love might experience itself as Lover and Beloved, is fulfilled; and union follows. And when union is attained, the Lover knows that he himself was all along the Beloved whom he loved and desired union with; and that all the impossible situations that he overcame were obstacles which he himself had placed in the path to himself.

To attain union is so impossibly difficult because it is impossible to become what you already are! Union is nothing other than knowledge of oneself as the Only One.

# 2

## *Wine and Love*

---

The Sufi Master-poets often compare love with wine. Wine is the most fitting figure for love because both intoxicate. But while wine causes self-forgetfulness, love leads to Self-realization.

The behaviour of the drunkard and the lover are similar; each disregards the world's standards of conduct and each is indifferent to the opinion of the world. But there are worlds of difference between the course and the goal of the two: the one leads to subterranean darkness and denial; the other gives wings to the soul for its flight to freedom.

The drunkenness of the drunkard begins with a glass of wine which elates his spirit and loosens his affections and gives him a new view of life that promises a forgetfulness from his daily worries. He goes on from a glass to two glasses, to a bottle; from companionship to isolation, from forgetfulness to oblivion— oblivion, which in Reality, is the Original State of God, but which, with the drunkard, is an empty stupor — and he sleeps in a bed or in a gutter. And he awakens in a dawn of futility, an object of disgust and ridicule to the world.

The lover's drunkenness begins with a drop of God's love which makes him forget the world. The more he drinks the closer he draws to his Beloved, and the more unworthy he feels of the Beloved's love; and he longs to sacrifice his very life at his Beloved's feet. He, too, does not know whether he sleeps on a bed or in a gutter, and becomes an object of ridicule to the world; but he rests in bliss, and God the Beloved takes care of his body and neither the elements nor disease can touch it.

One out of many such lovers sees God face to face. His longing becomes infinite; he is like a fish thrown up on the beach, leaping and squirming to regain the ocean. He sees God everywhere and in everything, but he cannot find the gate of union. The Wine that he drinks turns into Fire in which he continuously burns in blissful agony. And the Fire eventually becomes the Ocean of Infinite Consciousness in which he drowns.

# 3

## *Stages of Love*

---

When lust goes love appears; and out of love comes longing. In love there can never be satisfaction, for longing increases till it becomes an agony which ceases only in Union. Nothing but union with the Beloved can satisfy the lover.

The Way of Love is a continual sacrifice; and what gets sacrificed are the lover's thoughts of 'I', until at last comes the time when the lover says, 'O Beloved! will I ever become one with you and so lose myself forever? But let this be only if it is your Will.' This is the stage of love enlightened by obedience.

Now the lover continuously witnesses the glory of the Beloved's Will; and in the witnessing does not even think of union. He willingly surrenders his entire being to the Beloved, and has no thought of self left. This is the stage when love is illumined by surrender.

Out of millions, only one loves God; and out of millions of lovers, only one succeeds in obeying, and, finally, in surrendering his whole being to God the Beloved.

I am God personified. You who have the chance of being in my living presence are fortunate and blessed.

# 4

## *Gifts of Love*

---

Love is a gift from God to man.
Obedience is a gift from Master to man.
Surrender is a gift from man to Master.

One who loves desires the will of the Beloved.
One who obeys does the will of the Beloved.
One who surrenders knows nothing but the will
of the Beloved.

Love seeks union with the Beloved.
Obedience seeks the pleasure of the Beloved.
Surrender seeks nothing.

One who loves is the lover of the Beloved.
One who obeys is the beloved of the Beloved.
One who surrenders has no existence other than
the Beloved.

Greater than love is obedience.
Greater than obedience is surrender.
All three arise out of, and remain contained in,
the Ocean of divine Love.

# 5

## *Love of Woman and God*

---

A man loves a woman who is living in a distant place. His love causes him to be thinking of her all the time, and he cannot eat and he cannot sleep. His thoughts are only on his separation from her and he continually longs for her. When this longing becomes too great, he either goes to her or he compels her to come to him. This is called Ishk-e-Mijazi or physical love.

To love God one should think of God, long for God and suffer the fire of separation until one's longing reaches its utmost limits, and God the Beloved comes to the lover and his thirst is quenched in union with God. This love is called Ishk-e-Haqqiqi, and is a gift from God.

But one who obeys the Master who is One with God, need not suffer these things, for in obedience is the Grace of the Master.

# 6

## *God is Shy of Strangers*

God exists. If you are convinced of God's existence then it rests with you to seek Him, to see Him and to realize Him.

Do not search for God outside of you. God can only be found within you, for His only abode is the heart.

But you have filled His abode with millions of strangers and He cannot enter, for He is shy of strangers. Unless you empty His abode of these millions of strangers you have filled it with, you will never find God.

These strangers are your age-old desires — your millions of wants. They are strangers to God because want is an expression of incompleteness and is fundamentally foreign to Him who is All-sufficient and wanting in nothing. Honesty in your dealings with others will clear the strangers out of your heart.

Then you will find Him, see Him and realize Him.

# 7

## *Absolute Honesty*

---

Absolute honesty is essential in one's search for God (Truth). The subtleties of the Path are finer than a hair. The least hypocrisy becomes a wave that washes one off the Path.

It is your false self that keeps you away from your true Self by every trick it knows. In the guise of honesty this self even deceives itself. For instance your self claims, I love Baba. The fact is, if you really loved Baba you would not be your false self making the self-asserting statement! The self, instead of being effaced in love, believes and asserts, *I* love Baba. Isn't that self-deception?

How will you get rid of this false self? How will you give up this shadowy I-am-ness and get established in the I-Alone-Am or God-Alone-Is state? Hafiz* has given the answer: Firaq-o-Wasl che khahi, reza-e-doost talab. (O Lover! Separation and Union are none of your business. Seek only to resign yourself to the Will of the Beloved.)

Even the craving for union with the Beloved creates bindings. Therefore do not bother about separation or union; just love and love all the more. Then, as you love more and more you are able to resign yourself and your Path to the Perfect Master who is the Way; and you undergo a gradual change and your ego asserts itself less and less. Then whatever the Perfect Master tells you to do, you are able to carry out. In the begin-

*Hafiz : A Persian poet who was a Perfect Master.

[ 8 ]

ning the mind grumbles, Why should I obey someone? But Hafiz consoles the mind by saying, O Mind! this bondage to the Master alone can give eternal Freedom.

The chosen ones of the Perfect Master obey Him implicitly. He who becomes the perfect 'slave' becomes a Perfect Master.

# 8

## *Become Footless and Headless*

---

There are two kinds of experience: real and imitation. Just as it is difficult to distinguish an imitation from a real pearl, so it is difficult to distinguish between an imitation and a real spiritual experience.

When finally the Real Experience is gained, worldly things and circumstances cannot affect you. Once gained, the Real Experience is never lost; it is permanent. To get this Experience Hafiz has said, Become footless and headless.

What is meant by becoming footless and headless? It means implicitly obeying the Perfect Master: following His orders literally and not using your head to analyse their significance; doing only what He wants you to do — your feet moving at His command and your life being lived in the way of His love.

# 9

## *A Journey Without Journeying*

The succession of experiences that one goes through in the process of involution is called the Spiritual Path, and the going through them is likened to a journey. On one stage you hear melodious sounds and music that enchant and overwhelm you. On another stage you see wonderful visions in which most often you get lost. Such experiences are part and parcel of the Great Dream in Illusion, though together they may be called a real or super Dream compared with day to day experiences of the gross sphere.

The experiences are so innumerable and varied, that the journey appears to be interminable and the Destination is ever out of sight. But the wonder of it is, when at last you reach your Destination you find that you had never travelled at all! It was a journey from here to Here. As one Sufi expressed it, When I plucked the date (Fruit of Realization) I found the fruit was within me.

The journey seems infinitely long while you are passing through the dream-experiences of reincarnation and the six planes of involution, until finally you merge into yourself to emerge as Self. But the journey is after all no journey: it is simply the momentum of your urge to awaken from the Dream and get established in the reality of the God-state of Infinite Consciousness. To awaken means to *consciously* experience the sound-sleep State of God. When you *awake* you find that the Great Dream containing all

[ 11 ]

the varied illusory aspects of dreaming, has vanished for ever. Heaven and hell as well as all the planes vanish within your Self, to remain as nothing. In this Awakened State, there is no scope for anything besides you — the Self, the Existence eternal and infinite.

This is the only Experience worth experiencing and aspiring after. To gain this Experience you have to become as dust at the feet of the Perfect Master — which amounts to becoming as nothing. And, when you become absolutely nothing, you become Everything.

# 10

## *The Inquisitive and Doubting Man*

---

Once an inquisitive and doubting man went to Bayazid the Perfect Master and said, 'You, being Perfect, ought to know the thoughts of others. What am I thinking of just now?' Bayazid replied, 'You are thinking that which you ought not to have thought of, and asking that which you ought not to have asked. Had you come with an open mind and curbed tongue you would have received that which you ought to have received, instead of this well-deserved rebuke.'

# 11

## *Three Sorts of <u>Cheap</u> Experiences*

---

On a certain stage of the spiritual journey there is an experience in which all things to the aspirant's physical eyes gradually fade away leaving a void, facing which he feels fright or panic. But the next moment a lotus appears within the void. This experience is not enduring, the lotus disappears and all things begin to reappear.

There is another sort of experience which completely dazes the aspirant, so that all else is obliterated from his consciousness. It is a state of conscious coma. Even physically there is an abrupt halt, and whatever the posture of the body at the moment this experience begins, it is maintained until the experience wears off. For instance, if at the moment the hand is in a raised position, it will remain raised until the end of the coma which may be of a short duration or may last for years at a stretch.

There is yet another sort of experience. It is the experience of the fourth plane. Here Infinite Power is in one's hand and this entails great *risk* to the aspirant.*
After crossing the fourth plane, one kisses the threshold of God's Abode. But, as Hafiz has said, Just before the 'kiss' there is the vault of heaven (asman) where you feel all powerful, but the least misuse of that power will drag you to the dust.

So, on this spiritual path, there are three sorts of cheap experience. The experience of the first causes

*Details are given in *God Speaks,* by Meher Baba.

fright, of the second makes one dazed; and with the third is the risk of an immense fall.

The Perfect Master (Qutub) does not make one consciously pass through the planes. To grant intermediate experiences of the planes, is child's play to the Perfect Master. But the Perfect Master is not interested in giving a 'drop' — when He gives, He gives the 'Ocean'. For Him to do so, He expects from His disciples complete obedience in wholehearted love. When this is fulfilled, in one moment He raises the disciple to the highest level, which is the Experience of Infinite Consciousness of the state of I am God!

## 12

*Three Types of . . .*

---

DISCIPLES:

Those who do not give but ask.
Those who give but also ask.
Those who give and never ask.

SEEKERS:

The intellectual seeker.
The inspired seeker who is an intellectual.
The inspired seeker.

YOGIS:

Those who master Yogic exercises merely for occult powers.
Those who long for the Goal and also for occult powers.
Those who long for the Goal and give no thought to occult powers.

LOVERS:

The *mast** who loves and knows only God. He loses all consciousness of his body and surroundings, and is dead to himself and the world. For him only God exists.

The one who lives in the world, carries out his worldly duties and responsibilities a hundred percent, but is all the time conscious that everything is passing and only God exists. He loves God without others being aware of it.

The one who completely surrenders to the God-Man
*mast: One who is intoxicated with love for God.

(the Christ or Avatar). He no longer lives for himself, but for the God-Man. This is the highest and rarest type of lover.

RESIGNERS:

Those who do what the Master asks at all cost, but expect reward.

Those who do what the Master asks, sacrificing everything and not expecting reward; but they do it because their surrender to the Master demands it of them.

Those who have no thought of their surrender and are so completely resigned to the Master's Will that the question of how, why or when, never enters their minds. These are the 'fortunate slaves' that Hafiz advises us to become:

> Mazan ze choono-chera dam ke banda-e-muqbil;
> Ze jan qabul kunad har sukhan ke Sultan guft.

Befitting a fortunate slave, carry out every command of the Master without any question of why or what.

## 13

## *Do Not Seek and You Will Find*

---

'Seek and you shall find' has become such a common-place that spiritual aspirants have begun to wonder what it means. To them I say, Do not seek and you will find.

Do not seek material pleasure and you will find the spiritual treasure. This means, seek only God by not seeking material pleasures, and you will find God.

You can only seek God through self-denial. The spiritual treasure cannot be obtained by merely stretching out your hand for it. Only in the complete-ness of self-denial can the spiritual treasure become self-evident.

There are three ways of obtaining the spiritual treasure:

To earn it yourself by self-denial;

To receive it as a spontaneous gift from God given to His lover whose self has become effaced in the intensity of his longing for his Beloved;

To inherit it directly from the Perfect Master who bequeaths it to those who remain completely resigned to His will.

Therefore if you wish to find the treasure, stop seek-ing material pleasure. Seek the kingdom of Heaven by not seeking the kingdom of earth, and you will find it.

# 14

## *God Seeks*

---

The humour of the divine love-game is that the One
who is sought is Himself the seeker. It is the Sought
who prompts the seeker to ask, Where can I find Him
whom I seek? The seeker asking, Where is God? is
really God saying, Where indeed is the seeker!

## 15

## *The Pearl Diver*

---

*When I became a lover I thought I had gained the Pearl of the Goal; foolish I did not know that this Pearl lies on the floor of an ocean which has innumerable waves to be encountered and great depths to be sounded.*

— HAFIZ

In the beginning the seeker of Truth is like a man who, having heard that a priceless pearl is to be got from the depths of the ocean, goes down to the sea-shore and first admires the vastness of the ocean and then paddles and splashes about in the shallows and, intoxicated with this new excitement, forgets about the pearl.

Out of many who do this, one after a while, remembers his quest and learns to swim and starts to swim out.

Out of many who do this, one masters swimming and reaches the open sea; the others perish in the waves.

Out of many who master swimming, one begins to dive; the others in their enjoyment of mastery, again forget about the pearl.

Out of many who practise diving, one reaches the ocean bed and grasps the pearl.

Out of many who get hold of the pearl, one swims back up to the surface with it, the others stay stuck on the floor gazing with wonder at the pearl.

Out of many who swim up to the surface, one returns to the shore. This one is the Perfect Master (Qutub) and He shows His pearl to the others — the divers, the swimmers, the paddlers, and so encourages them in their efforts. But He can if He wishes cause another to become the possessor of the pearl without that one having to learn swimming and diving.

But God-Man or Avatar is the Master of Masters (Qutub-al-Aktab), and can give possession of the Pearl to any number he likes. The Qutub is perfect Perfection, but is circumscribed by His office in regard to His help to men. The Avatar is beyond limits of function; His power and the effects of His power are boundless. The absolute Perfection of the Perfect Master is the same as God-Man's. The difference between them is in the scope of their functioning. One is limited, the other is unlimited.

# 16

## *The Four Journeys*

God is Infinite and His Shadow is also infinite. The Shadow of God is the Infinite Space that accommodates the infinite Gross Sphere which, with its occurrences of millions of universes, within and without the range of men's knowledge, is the Creation that issued from the Point of Finiteness in the infinite Existence that is God.

In these millions of universes are many systems with planets: some in gaseous states, some in states of solidification, some which are Stone and Metal, some which also have Vegetation, some which also have developed life forms such as Worms, some also Fish, some also Birds, some also Animals, and a few also have Human Beings.

Thus it is that throughout the myriads of universes there are planets on which the "Seven Kingdoms" of Evolution are manifested; and the evolution of Consciousness and Forms is completed.

*But only on the planet Earth do human beings reincarnate and begin the Involutionary Path to Self Realization.*

Earth is the Centre of this Infinite Gross Sphere of millions of universes inasmuch as it is the Point to which all human-conscious souls must migrate in order to begin the Involutionary Path.

This Involutionary Path has seven Stations and arrival at the seventh Station completes the First Journey to God.

Although the completion of this Journey is the Goal of all human souls, only a very few at any given moment embark upon it. The arrival at the end of this Journey is the drowning of individuality in the Ocean of Infinite Consciousness, and the Journey's completion is the soul's absorption in the state of I-am-God with full consciousness, and, as God, experiences Infinite Power, Knowledge and Bliss.

Out of all the souls who complete the First Journey, a very few enter the Second Journey. This Journey has no stations. It is an instantaneous journey—the journey of infinite Consciousness being shaken from its absorption in I-am-God to abiding in God as God. In this state individuality is regained, but individuality is now infinite, and this Infinity includes Gross Consciousness, and so as Man and God he experiences Infinite Power, Knowledge and Bliss in the midst of Most-finiteness — the unlimited Soul knows Its unlimitedness in the midst of limitation.

The Third Journey is undertaken only by those who have accomplished the Second Journey and whose lot it is to bear the burden of the exercise of Infinite Power, Knowledge and Bliss and so live God's Life both as Man and God simultaneously.

There are only five such Masters living on the Earth at any given moment, and they control the movement of the universes and the affairs of the worlds of men. Only when one of these FIVE PERFECT MASTERS drops His body can one of those who are abiding in God as God move onwards and complete the Third Journey to fill the vacant Office.

It is the duty of these Five Perfect Masters to precipitate the Advent of the Ancient One (Avatar) and to hand over to Him the charge of His own Creation.

All those who live God's Life on Earth and all those

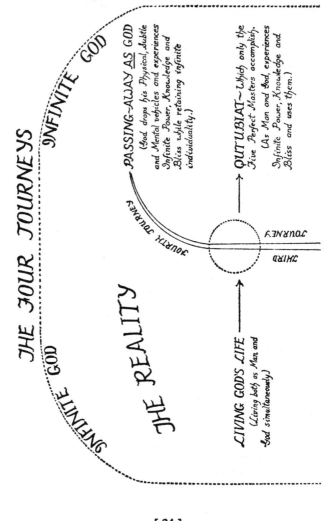

# THE FOUR JOURNEYS

**INFINITE GOD**

**INFINITE GOD**

**INFINITE GOD**

## THE REALITY

**PASSING-AWAY AS GOD**
(God drops his Physical, Subtle and Mental vehicles and experiences Infinite Power, Knowledge and Bliss while retaining infinite individuality.)

**OUT-U-BIAT**—Which only the Five Perfect Masters accomplish.
(As Man and God, experiences Infinite Power, Knowledge and Bliss and uses them.)

FOURTH JOURNEY

THIRD JOURNEY

**LIVING GOD'S LIFE**
(Living both as Man and God simultaneously.)

[ 24 ]

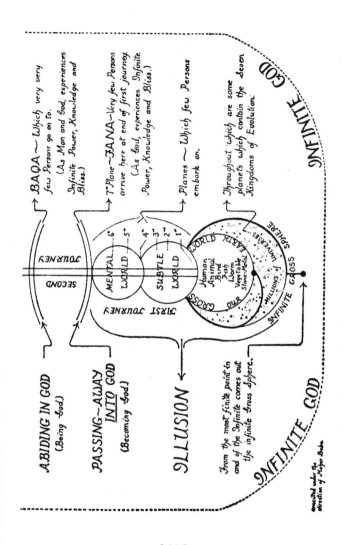

BAQA~ Which very very few Persons go on to.
(As Man and God, experiences Infinite Power, Knowledge and Bliss.)

7ᵗʰ Plane–FANA~Very few Persons arrive here at end of first journey. (As God, experiences Infinite Power, Knowledge and Bliss.)

Planes ~ Which few Persons embark on.

Throughout which are some planets which contain the seven Kingdoms of Evolution.

INFINITE GOD

MENTAL WORLD 6ᵗʰ 5ᵗʰ
SUBTLE WORLD 4ᵗʰ 3ʳᵈ 2ⁿᵈ 1ˢᵗ
EARTH WORLD
Human Animal Bird Fish Worm Vegetable Stone-Metal
OUR GROSS WORLD
MILLIONS of UNIVERSES
INFINITE GROSS SPHERE

SECOND JOURNEY
FIRST JOURNEY

ABIDING IN GOD
(Being God.)

PASSING–AWAY INTO GOD
(Becoming God.)

ILLUSION

From the most finite point in and of the Infinite comes out the infinite Gross Sphere.

INFINITE GOD

executed under the direction of Meher Baba.

who abide in God as God on Earth when they drop their bodies also shed forever their Subtle and Mental vehicles and pass away utterly as God, retaining infinite Individuality and experiencing Infinite Power, Knowledge and Bliss. This is the Fourth Journey.

In reality these Four Journeys are never journeyed, for God has nowhere to journey. He is without beginning and without end. And everything, which has the appearance of being, appeared from That which has no beginning and passes back into That which has no ending.

# 17

## *The Wine-seller*

Sufi poets use the figure of wine and its effects to describe the Way of Love and the condition of the lover. Saqi is the wine-seller, Rind is the customer and Maikhana is the wine-shop. Saqi-ul-Irshad is the vintner who makes and wholesales wine — the Wine-seller to the wine-sellers.

As in the world there are many wine-shops where new and unracked, and even adulterated, wine is sold for a small price, and which brings madness upon those who drink it and destroys their bodies and minds, so on the Spiritual Path there are saqis who have not let the wine of love they have got from the Saqi-ul-Irshad mature, but have used it straightway themselves to obtain the intoxication of cheap spiritual experiences, and even added pure spirits to it to increase its potency; and they sell it to anyone for the coins of small services.

And again, as there are wine-shops where only good vintage-wine is stocked for connoisseurs, so there are Saqis who are saints and perfect saints (walis and pirs) who have the mature wine of love for God alone, the price they have paid for which is the sacrifice of all that is near and dear; and this price they, in their turn, require from those who go to them.

Among those who have paid this price through many lives, one has the rare fortune to be invited by the Saqi-ul-Irshad to visit his cellar. And he gives this one a little glass from his special cask, and this overpowers him completely and he becomes merged with God. And

out of many such intimates he makes one as himself —
a Saqi-ul-Irshad.

The Saqi-ul-Irshad is the Qutub, the Perfect Master,
who is the Pivot of the Universe. He is All-power and
has the authority to use it as he wills. He never gives
one intoxication (masti), but causes one to see God face
to face, and some he makes one with God. As Hafiz
says:

> One who is Saqi-ul-Irshad can, with his mere
> glance or wish transform dust into the alchemy-
> stone that transmutes base metal into gold.

And sometimes it happens that there is one who has
served the Saqi-ul-Irshad faithfully in previous lives
and now has not even the price of the cheapest wine,
and the Master remembers him and calls him and gives
him the little drink of the Wine which gives Realization, and, perhaps, makes him a Saqi-ul-Irshad.

# 18

## *The Unlimited One is the Sadguru*

Kabir said:

> Kan fooka Guru Had ka Behad ka Guru nahee.
> Behad ka Sadguru hai soch samaj mana mahee.
> (The ear-whispering Guru is of the Limited; he is
> not of the Unlimited.
> Of the Unlimited is the Sadguru. Grasp this clearly
> in the mind.)

Although by 'ear-whispering' Kabir speaks specifically of the 5th plane Gurus, Gurus of the 6th plane may also be included as both are within the domain of the Limited.

We find three types of Gurus or Masters in the world at all times:

> The impostor;
> The genuine but limited Guru — the Wali or
> Master of the 5th plane and the Pir or Master
> of the 6th plane;
> The perfect Guru or Sadguru who is God-realized.

When a Wali is pleased with someone he whispers or breathes a divine Word in his ear, or he looks steadily into the eyes of the person concerned and causes a lift in that person's consciousness. In this heightened consciousness the person can easily read the thoughts of those near him if he wants to. He sees coloured lights and sometimes sees the face of the Wali within the light.

But the Wali may raise one to his own level of consciousness and cause him to identify himself with the mental body, and he sees his gross and subtle bodies distinctly as garments that he wears. Although this raising of another's consciousness is not mere hypnotism but bestowal of an experience of a very high order, the state enjoyed, being within the domain of limitation (Had), is still part of the passing-show of illusion. The angle of vision has merely shifted from what it was previously. The view is vastly greater, but he still faces Maya* with his back to God.

A Pir does not use either of the methods of the Wali. When he is pleased with someone he may ask for a glass of water or a cup of tea and taking a sip or two may give it to him to drink; or he may ask the person for something such as a handkerchief or scarf and after using it for some time return it to him. By such a seemingly insignificant action the Pir may bring him up through any of the lower planes, even to his own station and cause him to take a complete about-turn so that Maya is forever behind him and before him is the indescribable beauty and glory of God.

In his lifetime a Wali and a Pir can raise one person or at the most two persons to his own level of consciousness. A Pir cannot take anyone beyond the sixth plane, which denotes the very edge of Limitation. There is an abyss to be crossed between the sixth and the seventh planes of Consciousness — between the last point in Limitation and infinite Limitlessness, the Goal.

A Pir is himself in the realm of duality and therefore cannot take anyone to the Unitive state of Unlimited Consciousness; a Sadguru being beyond the bounds of Limitation, can and does do so. He utilizes infinite ways (including direct physical touch, or even just a wish)

*Maya: The Principle of Ignorance.

[ 30 ]

for the bestowing of His grace on the ones He chooses, to make them transcend duality and merge in the Consciousness of God the Unlimited (Behad).

A Wali or a Pir necessarily requires the physical presence of a person whose level of consciousness he intends to raise. But time and space are no obstacles to a Sadguru when he wishes to bestow His Grace on any person or thing. The person concerned may be thousands of miles away or not even in a physical body. Just a wish of the Sadguru can instantaneously establish that particular individual in the consciousness of the seventh plane of Limitlessness (Behad).

But where are these planes and spheres? They are all within you. You are not conscious of them because different states of consciousness give rise to different levels of consciousness. For example, take an ant as representing the first plane, a dog the third plane, an elephant the fifth plane and a man the seventh plane of consciousness. The ant, the dog, the elephant and the man move on the same earth, but there are worlds of difference in their levels of consciousness. The Limited and the Limitless lie within you. Rather they are you, but you do not experience them so because of the falseness attached to the Real 'I' which causes it to play the part of the false 'I'.

All upheavals are in the limitations of the consciousness. A Pir can make one see God, but even then one's real 'I' still has falseness attached to it. A Sadguru, at the right moment, whisks away entirely the entire falseness. And how does He do it? That is inexplicable. Only he who is Knowledge Itself can do this. When falseness is entirely shed, Real Individuality is established. This is the 'I am God' state.

The only way to get beyond the bounds of Limitation and get established in Limitlessness, is to become as dust in one's love for the Perfect Master. So Tukaram, one of the Perfect Masters, has said:

Sadguru vachoni sapday-ne soye,
Dharave-te paye adhee adhee.
Without the Grace of the Perfect Master you
    cannot find the way to the Goal;
Before and above everything else hold firmly to
    His feet.

# 19

## *The Divine Pretence*

Jesus had Christ-consciousness. This means that Jesus was conscious of Himself as Christ. Jesus the Christ was in Judas; and as Jesus the Christ in Judas He knew that Judas would betray Him. Yet He remained as though He knew nothing.

This divine Pretence of the All-knowing is the principle of His Leela — the Divine Sport of the eternal Christ.

# 20

## *A Plight*

---

The Soul's knowing that it knows everything is Dnyan
(Knowledge). Dnyan is the All-knowing experience of
the Soul. The Soul says, 'Now I know that I know
everything.' The All-knowing Soul's not knowing that
it knows, was pure imagination.

> Oh! you ignorant, All-knowing Soul,
>     what a plight you are in;
> Oh! you weak, All-powerful Soul,
>     what a plight you are in;
> Oh! you miserable, All-happy Soul,
>     what a plight you are in.

> What a plight!
> What a sight!
> What a delight!

# 21

## *Imparting of Knowledge*

Knowledge is imparted in two ways — indirectly and directly. There are two steps in the imparting of indirect Knowledge and two different ways in imparting direct Knowledge.

In order to make a clear picture let us liken gross-consciousness of the ordinary human-being to remote village-life, and God-consciousness of the realized-being to life in New York, and the six states of involution of consciousness to six halts or ports of call between the two places.

If you as a villager go to New York and remain there absorbed in the life of the city, you will not be able to tell those who have stayed in the village about your experience. But if you return to the village with your new knowledge, and, at the same time, remember the speech and ways of the villagers, you will be able to describe to them what you have seen and experienced, and so encourage some of them to make the journey also.

But you cannot sustain their interest indefinitely by description alone, so, through the aid of coloured slides and a projector you give them actual glimpses of New York. This brings Reality more vividly before the seekers' minds and spurs their interest to make the journey.

Now, there are two ways in which a villager can travel: either on his own under your directions, in which case he is exposed to the enchantments of each port of call — but his love and faith and full trust in you will save him from being ensnared and never completing the journey; or you may take him blindfolded under your personal care and he sees nothing until he reaches New York with you and you take the bandage from his eyes. This is the safer and quicker way. But whichever way, when he arrives at his destination he sees and experiences directly all the wonder and grandeur that he had only glimpsed on the screen.

The direct knowledge of God is that Knowledge (Dnyan) had through the experience of becoming one with God and can only be had by the grace of the Perfect Master. But indirect knowledge such as that obtained through descriptions and pictures is information for the mind only.

To know Reality is to become it. It is nearest to you — for, in fact, it is you. Owing to ignorance God who is nearest appears to be farthest. But when the veil of ignorance is rent by the grace of the Perfect Master you become you — the real Self which is the innermost Reality that you are, ever were and ever will be.

## 22

### *Types of Knowledge*

Knowledge is of three types:

1. *Material Knowledge*
(Bahaya Dnyan) of the external: comprises knowledge pertaining to worldly matters (affairs of the world), gained naturally or acquired through study. This knowing is ignorance of Ignorance.

2. *Spiritual Knowledge*
(Antar Dnyan) of the internal: comprises the spiritual experiences of the Subtle Planes and of the Mental Planes. Experiencing the Subtle Planes is ignorance of Knowledge. Experiencing the Mental Planes is knowledge of Ignorance. The inner experiences of the Subtle Planes may be said to be divine hallucination; while the inner experiences of the Mental Planes may be said to be a spiritual nightmare of longing for Union with God. Inner experiences end in Divine Awakening.

3. *Divine Knowledge*
(Brahma Dnyan) of Godhood: is God's own Infinite Knowledge. This is knowledge of the Knowledge.

    Bahaya Dnyan is mastered by a very few.
    Antar Dnyan is mastered by very, very few.
    Brahma Dnyan is attained by a rare one.

The Brahma-Dnyani is All-knowing and All-knowledge, for He has become the Source of Knowledge and is Knowledge Itself.

# 23

## *Introductions*

---

As a rule an introduction is required between people who do not know one another. Such introduction is not felt to be necessary when there is a give and take of love between persons, for hearts need no introduction. An affinity can be felt between strangers, a feeling of having known one another before. This feeling is because of their connections in previous lives.

No one requires an introduction to me, for no one is a stranger to me. However, I am a stranger to most, and those coming and remaining in my presence do not do so without introduction. As a matter of fact, they have come with many introductions—for many times in previous lives have they been introduced to me and have gone away and forgotten me and met me again. All these introductions are their introduction to me this time.

# 24

## *Sahavas Sayings*

Love is such that the lover needs no asking to do anything.

* * *

By loving, your whole being will be changed and your life will end in Freedom.

* * *

The gift of love is a rare gift of God, and rarely is one capable of receiving it.

* * *

God is infinitely more vital to your existence than your breath which is your very life. Ordinarily, life is associated with breath; but you only become aware of this when breath is restricted through exertion, and you only completely realize this when breath is cut off altogether as when drowning. Similarly, you only become aware that God is your existence when you pant for Him, and you only finally realize Him when you drown in His Ocean of divine Love.

* * *

It is difficult for one to understand the Spiritual Path, and still more difficult to get *on* the Path.

* * *

What is fasting the mind? It is having no thoughts. But this is impossible. But when you entrust your mind to me by constantly remembering me, there are no thoughts left on which the mind can feed. This fasting is the true and essential fasting. Starving the stomach may benefit the health but it does not necessarily help spiritual advancement.

*    *    *

You say that you see me in dreams. These dreams arise from your own impressions formed through your love and faith in me. Do not attribute them to me. I have come into your midst to awaken you from the long, drawn-out Dream of Illusion — not to create more dreams for you!

# 25

## *Do Not Absent Yourself*

---

He who has eyes but does not see,
He who has ears but does not hear,
He who has a tongue but does not speak,
He can see Me as I should be seen, and can
     know Me as I should be known.

This does not mean that you should become inactive. On the contrary it means that you should be constantly alert towards the expressive Beauty of the All-pervading Beloved. On this Hafiz has said, If you want your Beloved to be present, do not absent yourself for one moment from His Presence.

The Perfect Master is in everything, and is the Centre of everything. Every one and every thing is therefore equidistant from Him. Though, owing to our own limitations, He appears outwardly to be present at only one place at a time, He is on every plane of consciousness at one and the same time. To see Him as He is, is to see God.

So beware lest when the divine Beloved knocks at the door of your heart He finds you absent.

# 26

## *Want What I Want*

I am God — God the Beyond and God in human form.
I draw you ever closer to me by giving you frequent
occasions of my companionship. But familiarity often
makes you forget that I am God.

I know all that happens and will happen. Whatever
happens does not happen without my will. Knowingly
I allow things to happen in their natural course.

All I ask of you is that you love me most and obey
me at all times. Knowing that it is impossible for you
to obey me as you should, I help you to carry out whole-
heartedly what I give you to do by repeatedly bringing
to you the importance of obedience.

Always do what I want, instead of wanting me to
want what you want. Most of you want me to want
what you want; and when you succeed in getting me
to agree to what you want you are delighted and even
tell others that that is what I want! For example, one
of you brings a youth to me saying, Baba, this is so
and so. He is a double graduate and would be an
excellent match for my daughter who is also a double
graduate. I need your approval. When I do not approve,
you persist saying, But Baba, he really is a good boy
and would suit my daughter very much. So I say, Is
that so? All right — approved! And as soon as you
step out of the room you start telling others that I want
your daughter to marry that youth. This sort of thing
is common with most of you. When I approve of what
you want to do, you say, It is what Baba wants me to

[ 42 ]

do. Be honest and careful in what you say. What I want of you is that you try your best to want what Baba wants.

I know it is not easy to want what I want. In fact, it is impossible for you to want what I want, for it is impossible for you to love me as I should be loved. But at least, do not always be wanting me to want what you want, and try your utmost to put your heart and soul into doing whatever I want you to do.

Only intense love for me can bring you to obey me as I *want* you to.

## 27

### *Your Gift of Obedience*

---

Let your heart be pure. Do not act outwardly what you are not inwardly. Be absolutely honest. God is Infinite Honesty.

Do not pose as being pious, because God is everywhere. God cannot be fooled — so why pose as something you are not?

I do not want anything else from you but the gift of your obedience. Give me that and you will free yourself from the bondage of ignorance.

# 28

## *The Divine Response*

---

The moment you try to understand God rather than love Him you begin to misunderstand Him, and your ignorance feeds your ego. Mind cannot reach that which is beyond it. God is infinite and beyond the reach of Mind.

The Divine Will that brought forth this infinite Illusion expresses itself in all its purity through me to make you turn away from Illusion towards God-consciousness.

Every moment I respond to the whole of creation. My response, being divine, is wholly from love. The many faces of that one response as you see them, are but the reflections of your many-mirrored mind. You view and judge my actions from your level of understanding and attempt to differentiate them in the light of your own limited standards of values. And so you misinterpret the different shades of my response to different people. Being unlimited I am simultaneously on all levels of consciousness; and, as such, in my response I differentiate one from the other solely in the light of their impressions (sanskaras), or the different states of consciousness that the impressions give rise to. Each action of mine is a response in accordance with the necessity of the recipients on various planes of consciousness. And so by its very nature and magnitude my divine response sometimes appears enigmatic.

Do not try with your limited mind to understand the significance of my actions, nor try to imitate them. You must not do what I do, but do what I tell you to do. To try to bring my every action within the orbit of your understanding is but to understand the limitations of your own understanding!

At times when I see you confused I am moved by my compassion and love for you to give an explanation of the reason for a particular action of mine. And so it seems that I am defending my actions by giving explanations for them. And thus is shown your weakness and my strength.

But remember that despite my explaining the significance of my actions, they will ever remain beyond the range of your knowing. The utter simplicity of my divine Game appears to be highly intricate as soon as you try to *understand* it through your intellect.

The more you have of my company and receive of my love with an open heart the more whole-heartedly you begin to accept me. And the more you see of me the more convinced you become that you understand me less and less. Exerting yourself to comprehend my divine Game through the process of understanding opens up vast fields of speculation in which you wander and arrive sooner or later at a dead-end, finding yourself hopelessly lost.

If my actions cause confusion it is because of your lack of complete trust. Therefore uproot all doubt and remember well that whatever I do is for the best. All my actions are my divine response born of my divine love.

# 29

## *The Questioning Mind*

Your love and faith has drawn you from hundreds of miles to be with me for a few hours. Although I sent you word that you should not ask me any questions I know that some of you are just waiting for the opportunity to ask some. It is the nature of the mind to go on asking. But love asks no questions; it seeks nothing but the will of the Beloved.

Mind wants to know that which is beyond mind. To know that which is beyond mind, mind must go — vanish, leaving no vestige of itself behind. The humour of it is, the mind, which is finite, wants to retain itself and yet know Truth, which is infinite. This is the position of those who seek Truth through intellect. Few grasp this fact, and so most grope and grapple in vain.

It is easy to ask questions, but it needs past preparation to grasp what I explain. Those who have the authority to ask and the capacity to understand do not ask. They understand that God is un-understandable and beyond the reach of the questioning mind.

Every one wants to be happy. Each of you seeks happiness in one way or another invariably to meet with dissatisfaction and disappointment. In reality you are Bliss itself — but what a comedy Illusion stages before you, what game it makes of you to make you aware of it!

One of my lovers has complained, Baba, I have led a pure life yet I have had to suffer much. Perhaps others of you have a similar complaint; but you can only have such because you have no idea of the purpose behind it all. I do not mean that you should invite suffering; I mean, do not fear suffering or blame anyone for it.

According to the Law that governs the universe, all suffering is your labour of love to unveil your Real Self. In comparison to the Infinite Bliss you experience on attaining the I-am-God state, all the suffering and agony you go through amounts to practically nothing. I am the Source of Infinite Bliss. To draw you to me and to make you realize that you are Bliss Itself, I come amidst you and suffer infinite agony.

I am the Ancient One. When I say I am God it is not because I have thought about it and concluded that I am God — I know it to be so. Many consider it blasphemy for one to say he is God; but in truth it would be blasphemous for me to say I am not God.

When you say, I am man, it is not a matter of possibly or perhaps. There is no doubt in your mind. No corroboration is needed and no contradiction could affect it. It is a matter of supreme certainty to you. Suppose you could descend to the level of animal consciousness while at the same time retaining human consciousness, what you would convey to the animal is, I am a man. I am a man and one day you too shall become man. I have come down to your level of consciousness while retaining Infinite Consciousness; and I repeatedly tell you that I am God in order to help you know that you too are God. I am God and everyone and everything is nothing but God, and one day everyone and everything too will become God consciously.

The greatest sin is hypocrisy. He is the greatest hypocrite, who, himself being one, asks others not to be hypocritical. I want you all to be honest. You should not pretend to be what you are not.

One of you has said, Baba, I am doing my duty honestly, yet I am not happy. Who is to be blamed for this? Does God take advantage of my weakness? I am happy with your frankness, but you have yet to come to that honesty which will show you that you cannot blame anyone for your condition. Whatever you want to be, that you become. However, if you want to blame anyone blame me, for everything in the universe has come out of me and so I am the only one who can be blamed. But you have no idea of my love and compassion which sustains your very being. In love is infinite compassion, and whatever happens is already tempered by compassion. You cannot understand this unless you go beyond the reach of mind.

If at all I did take advantage of your weakness it would be only for your advantage. Weakness is but a degree of strength. As Infinite Life I experience myself as everyone and everything; I enjoy and suffer through you to make you aware that you are Infinite.

Why should you not be happy? What need bind you to unhappiness? Binding is self-created. It can be overcome if you really want to become free. You are your own obstacle to freedom, and merely wishing for freedom is not enough. It is not what you think or say that matters, but what you sincerely feel within. If you want God, you must want God *alone*. It is possible to get God if you *want* to experience Truth. And what is the cost? Your own separate existence. When you surrender all falseness you inherit the Truth that you really *are*.

Truth is beyond the reach of mind. It is a matter of experience. Mind is very elusive and creates innumerable excuses in order to entrap you. It causes you to say, I cannot live just for God. I have my duty towards my family, towards society, the nation and the world.

[ 49 ]

And so you are pulled more into Illusion than towards Truth.

Truth is simple, but Illusion makes it infinitely intricate. The person is rare who possesses an insatiable longing for Truth; the rest allow Illusion to bind them ever more and more. God alone is Real and all else that you see and feel is nothing but a series of nothings.

I am Infinite Knowledge, Power and Bliss. I can make anyone realize God if I choose to do so. You may ask, Why not make me realize God now? But why should it be you? Why not the person next to you or the man in the street, or that bird on the tree, or that stone — who are all one in different forms? The more you love me the sooner you will discard the falsehood you have chosen to hide under that hoodwinks you into believing you are what you are not. I am in all and love all equally. Your love for me will wear through your falseness and make you realize the Self that you truly are.

Mere intellectual understanding does not bring God nearer to you. It is love, not questioning, that will bring God to you. Questioning nourishes pride and separateness. So do not ask questions, but strive to become a 'slave' of the Perfect Master.

When your life presents an honest and sincere picture of your mind and heart just an embrace from a Perfect Master is enough to quicken the spirit. When I the Ancient One embrace you I awaken something within you which gradually grows. It is the seed of Love that I have sown. There is a long period and great distance between the breaking open of the seed and its flowering and fruiting. Actually the Goal is neither far nor near and there is no distance to cross nor time to count. In Eternity all is *here* and *now*. You have simply to become that which you are. You are God, the Infinite Existence.

[ 50 ]

## 30

*Awake Dream State to Real Awake State*

---

The First Song of the Infinite is the beginning of Creation. It brings about the apparent descent of the Infinite into the domain of multiple duality. Duality implies unending sufferings.

I am eternally happy for I know that I am the Infinite One. I alone exist; there is nothing besides me; all else is Illusion. Simultaneously, I suffer eternally.

I, as myself, am free. But in you, as you, I get myself bound. I knowingly suffer through you, to make you free from bindings. This is my crucifixion. Your experience of suffering is because of sheer ignorance; and your ignorance is my suffering.

You are sitting here before me, each one asserting his separate existence from the other. You come from different levels of society. You possess varied physical and mental aptitudes and abilities. Through the ego-mind you have become individualized, and the One Indivisible Soul is infinitely divided. But the Soul never becomes divided, it ever remains One and the Same.

You are really the Infinite Soul but you identify yourself with a finite mind and so have to suffer. You have your moments of happiness and sorrow. Whether your pains outweigh your pleasures or your pleasures outweigh your pains, you worry all day about something or the other until your finite existence retreats at night into sound sleep. There you unconsciously merge in the Infinite.

In sound sleep you completely forget yourself and

your surroundings, your thoughts and emotions around which are ranged your ideas of imagined happiness and sufferings. But this respite is short-lived.

From the sound-sleep state you come down to the normal awake state, and as you come you have necessarily to pass through a dream state even though it be for only the fraction of a second.

Now, at one time you have a very happy and sweet dream in which your ideal of happiness is fulfilled. But being a dream it lasts only a little while, and waking pains you so much that you sigh, What a pity it was only a dream!

At some other time you have a horrible dream in which you experience great suffering. Time seems an eternity. As you wake you feel such relief that you say, Thank God it was only a dream after all.

In the dream state you enjoy and suffer. When you wake you realize that your enjoyment and suffering was nothing but a dream — an illusion. But know that your present state of consciousness which you call being awake, when compared to the Real Awake State, is nothing but a dream state. Your life is a dream within the mighty Dream of God which is the Universe.

From your present awake dream state you have to go through many sleeps of deaths before you get established in the Real Awake State. After ordinary sleep you awake in the same surroundings; after death you arise in a new environment. But this does not bring the end of your suffering, for the Thread of Action (Karma) continues unbroken and unfailingly keeps on determining your life. The humour of it is new settings create new worries. The grip of illusion is so tight and deceitful that you cannot help worrying. So your life in your awake dream state becomes an endless chain of suffering.

You, as gross body, are born again and again till you realize your Real Self. You, as mind, are born only once and die only once; in this sense you do not re-incarnate. The gross body keeps changing, but mind (mental body) remains the same throughout. All impressions (sanskaras) are stored in the mind. The impressions are either to be spent or counteracted through fresh karma in successive incarnations. Buddha's wheel denotes the cycle of births and deaths. The wheel goes on in its ceaseless round. It lifts you to the heights; it brings you down to the depths.

To show you how karma persists as a connecting link and a life-determining factor of future lives I give you an example. There is a king who has vast possessions. But he is a worthless king. He spends all his energy and money in selfish pursuits and luxuries and has no care for his subjects. In his next birth he is born blind and becomes a beggar and thus compensates for his wrong doings.

Now this king has a servant who is honest and faithful and hard-working. In his next birth because of his merits he is born into a cultured and well-to-do family. One day, when he is going along the street he hears a pitiable cry from the pavement. It is from the blind beggar who was the king in his previous life crying aloud with outstretched hands, Have pity. Give me a penny in the name of the Lord. And because all actions however trivial, are inwardly determined by the Sanskaric ties, creating claims and counter-claims, the rich man is unconsciously drawn towards the beggar and gives him a few copper coins. A king crying out for alms and a servant taking pity on him—what a comedy, what an irony of fate! This is the working of the law of karma, the expression of justice in the world of values. The law of karma is impartial and inexorable.

It knows no concessions, gives no preferences, makes no exceptions. It dispenses justice.

By the divine law you are shielded from remembrance of past lives, for it would not help you in living your present life but would make it infinitely more complicated and confusing.

For me 'past' does not exist. I live in the Eternal Present. I clearly see your former lives, with all your intimate and intricate relationships with so many individuals. Your various reactions to others seen in the context of your mutual connections in previous lives serves as a mighty joke to me and helps to ease my burden of suffering.

Now, I give you another example. It is not an uncommon happening. A Moslem after death is buried in a graveyard. After a few incarnations he is born again in a Moslem family in the same town. It is customary among Moslems to offer prayers for the dead when they visit graves, to pray to God Almighty to save the departed ones. And so it happens that this person stands before his own grave and solemnly prays, 'May God save his soul!' What an absurdity! how pathetic!

The wheel of births and deaths ceaselessly turns. You are born as a male, as a female; rich, poor; brilliant, dull; healthy, weak; black, white; of different nationalities and of different creeds, in accordance with your inherent and imperative need to have that richness of experience which helps transcend all forms of duality. Side by side with the experience, the paying and receiving of payment of karmic debts go on ad infinitum. How can you clear the account? The Avatar, or the Sadguru, having universal Mind, literally embodies universal life. It is through Him that you become free from this business of karma.

The life of everything and everyone is an open book

[ 54 ]

to me. It is like a film show that I enjoy at my own cost. I am the sole Producer of this ever-changing and never-ending film called the universe, wherein I become you in your awake dream state in order to awaken you to the Real Awake State. When you experience this state you will realize the nothingness of what was your awake dream state which you experience now. This needs my Grace. When my Grace descends it makes you Me.

# 31

## *I Am Infinite Consciousness*

Believe that I am the Ancient One. Do not doubt that for a moment. There is no possibility of my being anyone else. I am not this body that you see. It is only a coat I put on when I visit you. I am Infinite Consciousness. I sit with you, play and laugh with you; but simultaneously I am working on all planes of existence.

Before me are saints and perfect saints and masters of the earlier stages of the spiritual path. They are all different forms of me. I am the Root of every one and every thing. An infinite number of branches spread out from me. I work through, and suffer in and for, each one of you.

My bliss and my infinite sense of humour sustain me in my suffering. The amusing incidents that arise at the expense of none lighten my burden.

Think of me; remain cheerful in all your trials and I am with you helping you.

# 32

## *I Am the Song*

---

My unique experience of the Beyond State is so unique that I simultaneously experience being everything and beyond everything. I am the song, its words and its melody, and I am the singer. I am the musical instruments and the players and the listeners. And on your level I explain to you the meaning of what I, the singer, sing.

# 33

## *Infinite Knowledge*

---

There cannot be anything hidden from the One who is everywhere present, for He is everywhere. And it naturally follows that when there cannot be anything hidden from this One He must also be All-knowing, knowing everything.

The infinite-Knowing is 'seeing' everything at one and the same time, and seeing it NOW. It is that Knowledge which does not begin and does not end; which is indivisible and continuous, and to which nothing can be added and from which nothing can be subtracted.

It is that Knowledge which makes God at this moment know that which He knew when it occurred countless aeons ago, and makes Him know that which will occur countless aeons hence; that Knowledge which makes everything known to God simultaneously and NOW. It is the Knowledge of the Perfect Masters and the Avatar.

In terms simpler to you it means that which you as individuals know at this moment I knew aeons ago, and what you as individuals in ages to come will be knowing at a particular moment, I know now.

# 34

## *Universal Body*

---

God's Imagination begets Universal Mind, Universal Energy and Universal Body in which are contained the individual minds, individual energies and individual bodies of every thing and being in Creation.

Universal Mind, Universal Energy and Universal Body are because of the existence of God's Imagination which exists as Non-existence within the Infinite Eternal and All-pervading EXISTENCE (God).

Individual minds, individual energies and individual bodies have no existence in themselves, but exist only as effects in existing Non-existence.

In my Universal Body are contained all the gross bodies of all the innumerable beings and things in Creation. Individual subtle bodies (energies) and mental bodies (minds) are part of my Universal Energy and Universal Mind. In both Universal Energy and Universal Mind there are no divisions.

Distance between a drop here and a drop there in the ocean makes no difference to each drop's relation to the ocean. Any drop within the ocean is within the entirety and homogeneity of the ocean.

There are no divisions in Paramatma; only the One Indivisible Ocean of Reality exists as Eternal Existence.

## 35

## *To Know Everything in a Flash*

How do I know everything? The nature of the infinitely complicated phenomenon — the Universe — is infinitely simple. But to know and understand this is infinitely difficult. When you know what Universal Mind, Universal Energy and Universal Body are and what their relation is to individual mind, individual energy and individual body you will understand how the Perfect Master knows everything.

This all-comprehensive Knowledge is obtained in a flash. But to know everything in a flash takes an eternity in the illusion of time while you gradually die to your self. This dying to your self means completely losing yourself in God to find your Self as God.

This dying to your false self is no easy task; raising a corpse to life is child's play compared to it.

# 36

## *Knowing and Not Knowing*

Being the highest and becoming the lowest I manifest Knowledge and assume ignorance at the same time.

Even though I know a certain thing will happen within a month, I may chalk out plans as if it was not to occur for years. Again, knowing that an event will not take place for years, I appear to expect it to happen shortly.

In Dnyan (Knowledge) there is Adnyan (Non-knowledge or Ignorance). But in Adnyan there cannot be Dnyan. Having all knowledge on the highest level, I can assume full ignorance on your level. In fact I am Infinite Knowledge, and as such I know what is to happen even after hundreds of years, yet I profess ignorance while I am on your level.

Even on the gross plane and in ordinary circumstances knowledge and ignorance can be manifested simultaneously. For instance, you say: I do not know how to swim. This implies that you know that you do not know how to swim. Were you not to know that you do not know, you could not have had this understanding. This is 'knowledge of ignorance'.

In the same way, I who am Knowledge itself manifest ignorance of knowledge. Knowing all, I seem not to know, at one and the same time.

# 37

## *Will and Worry*

---

Duality implies separateness. Separateness causes fear. Fear makes worry.

The way of Oneness is the way to happiness; the way of manyness is the way to worry.

I am the one who has no second so I am eternally happy. You are separate from your Self, so you always worry.

To you, what you see is absolutely real; to me it is absolutely false.

I alone am Real and my will governs the cosmic illusion. It is the truth when I say that the waves do not roll and the leaves do not move without my will.

The moment the intensity of your faith in my will reaches its height you say goodbye to worry forever. Then, all that you suffered and enjoyed in the past, together with all that you may experience in the future, will be to you the most loving and spontaneous expression of my will; and nothing will ever be able to cause you worry again.

Live more and more in the Present which is ever beautiful and stretches away beyond the limits of the past and the future.

If at all you must worry, let it be how to remember me constantly. This is worthwhile worry because it will bring about the end of worry.

Think of me more and more, and all your worries will disappear into the nothing they really are. My will works out to awaken you to this.

[ 62 ]

# 38

## *The Jest on My Chest*

---

As the Highest of the High I am the Wisest of the Wise, yet I have allowed myself to perform an act more foolish than any fool ever would. What is this foolish act of mine? Creating the CREATION.

Creation is really a mighty joke, but the laugh is at my own expense — and now the jest is proving a burden on my chest. Sometimes I am so tired I feel like going to sleep for 700 years.

To the fool a foolish act is most natural and effortless. But can you imagine the Most Wise exerting himself and stretching out to perform an act which is opposite to his attribute of Wisdom! That is why I say you can have no idea of what I mean when I say I am tired — it is beyond human understanding.

# 39

## Knowledge

The Sadguru has not to know, He knows.
He knows that there is nothing to know.

## Purposes

There are some who exist to hate others, be jealous of others and make others unhappy; and there are some who exist to love others and make others happy. One who has become One with God, exists for all, both good and bad. And to become One with God, one has not to renounce anything but one's own self.

## Meaning

Understanding has no meaning.
Love has meaning.
Obedience has more meaning.
Holding my 'daman'* has most meaning.

## Suffering

I know three things:
I am the Avatar in every sense of the word.
Whatever I do is the expression of my unbounded love.
I suffer infinite agony eternally through your ignorance.

*'daman': dress.

# 40

## *Maya the Showman*

Maya, the Master-illusionist who produces seemingly existent worlds out of Nothing, will perform its master trick of making everything including my health, energy, words and promises apparently go against me; and my lovers' faith and trust in me will be tested to their full extent. But Maya is powerless to go against my Work — for Maya itself is the means by which I bring about the results of my Work.

Being the instrument for the fulfilment of my Work, Maya, in fact, actually does its utmost to bring about the utmost results of this Work. Maya is the infinite shadow of God's infinity, and so, having no existence except in non-existence, must naturally give way to the one and only Reality which is God. And then God manifests in His glory.

When the sun appears over the horizon the shadow projected by an object is much bigger than the object, but when the sun is directly overhead the shadow is under the feet as it were of the object.

In my present phase of helplessness and humiliation, the Sun of Truth's rays appear faint and feeble and the Shadow of Maya large. But when that Sun will be at its zenith the Shadow that was cast ahead of Man, and which dominated his vision and thought will disappear. This will be the victory over Maya when ignorance will be effaced in the glory of God's manifestation through me.

Keep your faces turned towards the Sun and your

shadow of individualized Maya will lie behind you and, though still existent, will have no power over you. But if you turn your backs to the Sun your shadows will be before you and you will be following them. Although of yourselves you cannot get rid of your shadows, if you turn your backs on them and keep facing the Sun, at the time of His full ascendance and glory your shadows will disappear forever.

# 41

## *At the Junction of Reality and Illusion*

---

The time I have been hinting at has come. The universal work weighs tremendously on me. *Maya*, the principle of ignorance, in full power tries to oppose my Work. So, particularly those who live near me must be very watchful. Knowing my love for you, Maya awaits an opportunity to use your weaknesses. The moment you neglect my instructions, Maya's purpose is served. I have to put up a big fight with Maya — not to destroy it, but to make you aware of its nothingness. The moment you fail to obey me implicitly it tightens its grip over you and you fail to carry out the duties given. This adds to my suffering.

In God there is no such thing as confusion — God is infinite Bliss and Honesty. In Illusion there is confusion, misery and chaos. As the eternal Redeemer of humanity I am at the junction of Reality and Illusion, simultaneously experiencing the infinite bliss of Reality and the suffering of Illusion.

With Reality on the one hand and Illusion on the other, I constantly experience as it were, a pull on either side. This is my crucifixion. When you fall a prey to the persuasions of Maya, the pull of Illusion is intensified and I have to exert myself to withstand it and remain stationed at the junction. I do not ever let go my hold on Reality. If the pull of Illusion becomes too great my arm may be pulled out of its socket, but I will remain where I am.

**42**

## *A Nod of My Head*

---

The word 'qutub' literally means 'pivot' or 'axis'. Thus the Qutub (Perfect Master) is the Axis around which everything in Creation revolves; and He being the CENTRE of everything, everything on every plane is equidistant from Him.

All action from you, as individuals or isolated points in consciousness stationed on different planes, is limited in expression and result. As the Centre, each movement of mine is unlimited in its action and reaction, expression and result.

For instance, a nod of your head in reply to different questions can indicate different actions and moods such as I am happy, I am miserable, I have eaten, I have rested, etc. But each nod expresses and conveys only one thing at a time. Whereas, as the Centre, one nod-of-my-head gives rise to a wave of innumerable actions and reactions simultaneously on all planes of consciousness.

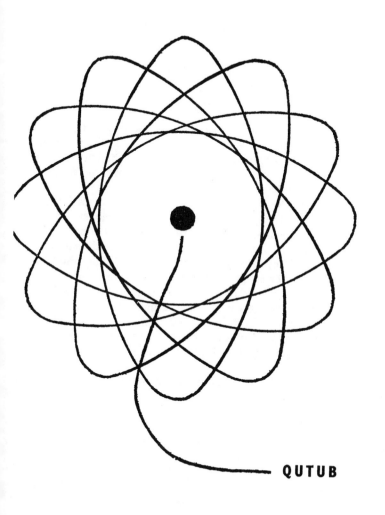

QUTUB

[ 69 ]

# 43

## *Toys in the Divine Game*

---

The Infinite alone exists and is Real; the finite is passing and false.

The Original Whim in the Beyond caused the apparent descent of the Infinite into the realm of the seeming finite. This is the Divine Mystery and the Divine Game in which Infinite Consciousness for ever plays on all levels of finite consciousness.

I am Infinite Consciousness, inter-penetrating and transcending all states of limited consciousness. The most primal and the most final categories of consciousness — say a stone or a saint — are equidistant from me, so I am equally approachable by all. I am the Way.

Unwavering loyalty to the Way is the real remedy for the sickness of impressioned consciousness. Some of my lovers, owing to fluctuating faith, fail to understand this and run hither and thither for Freedom. For me it then becomes a matter of retrieving them, and others wonder why I give so much attention to these people.

A child has many toys, and it likes to play with some more than with others, and one is so dear that he won't part with it even when he goes to bed. If someone snatches away a favourite toy he must get it back, and if one gets broken he demands that it be mended; he will not be consoled with another even more costly one.

It is the same with me. I am a child whose playground is the universe. All beings and things are my toys in my divine Game — compared with my being and power all are inanimate toys — but they are toys which I inspire with my life-giving love.

All are equally me and I reside in each always, but some are dearer to me, and if one of these is taken from me I must get him back. And others have no right to wonder why I show so much concern for this one.

## 44

## *God Alone Is*

---

Infinite consciousness is infinite. It can never lessen at any point in time or space. Infinite consciousness being infinite includes every aspect of consciousness. Unconsciousness is one of the aspects of infinite consciousness. Thus infinite consciousness includes unconsciousness. It sustains, covers, pierces through and provides an end to unconsciousness — which flows from, and is consumed by, infinite consciousness.

I assert unequivocally that I am infinite consciousness; and I can make this assertion because I *am* infinite consciousness. I am everything and I am beyond everything.

I am ever conscious that I am you, while you are never conscious that I am in you. Daily I support you and share your consciousness. Now I want you to uphold me, so that one day you can share my consciousness.

For man, unconscious of actually possessing the never-ending continuously conscious experience that God is everything and *all else* is nothing, everything is everything. Air is. Water is. Fire is. Earth is. Light is. Darkness is. Stone is. Iron is. Vegetation is. Insect is. Fish is. Bird is. Beast is. Man is. Good is. Bad is. Pain is. Pleasure is. There is no end to what is — until he arrives at *nothing is* and instantaneously he realizes *God Is*.

It is not easy for man to accept and keep on accepting under all circumstances that God is. Even after his firm acceptance that God is, it is supremely difficult, though not impossible, for him to *realize* what he has firmly accepted. And realization means that instead of being fully conscious that he is man, he becomes fully conscious that he is God, was God, has always been God and will ever remain God.

Knowingly or unknowingly man is ever seeking the Goal, which is to realize his true Self. The very nearest and innermost to man is his Soul, but the humour of it is he feels far, far away from It. There appears to be no end to his journeys towards the Goal through the numberless highways and by-ways of life and death, although in fact there is no distance at all to cover. Having achieved full consciousness as man, he has already arrived at his destination, for he now possesses the capacity to become fully conscious of his Soul. Still he is unable to realize this divine destiny because his consciousness remains completely focussed on his inverted, limited, finite self — the Mind — which, ironically, has been the means of achieving consciousness.

Before he can know Who he is, man has to unlearn the mass of illusory knowledge he has burdened himself with on the interminable journey from unconsciousness to consciousness. It is only through love that you can begin to unlearn, and, eventually, put an end to all that you do not know. God-love penetrates all illusion, while no amount of illusion can dim God-love. Start learning to love God by beginning to love those whom you cannot. You will find that in serving others you are serving yourself. The more you remember others with kindness and generosity, the less you remember yourself; and when you completely forget yourself, you find me as the Source of all Love.

Give up all forms of parrotry. Start practising whatever you truly feel to be true and justly to be just. Do not make a show of your faith and beliefs. You have not to give up your religion, but to give up clinging to the husk of mere ritual and ceremony. To get to the fundamental core of Truth underlying all religions, reach beyond religion.

Through endless time God's greatest gift is continuously given in silence. But when mankind becomes completely deaf to the thunder of His Silence God incarnates as Man. The Unlimited assumes limitation to shake Maya-drugged humanity to a consciousness of its true destiny. He uses a physical body for His universal work, to discard it in final sacrifice as soon as it has served its purpose.

God has come again and again in various Forms, has spoken again and again in different words and different languages the Same One Truth — but how many are there that live up to it? Instead of making Truth the vital breath of his life, man compromises by making over and over again a mechanical religion of it — a handy staff to lean on in times of adversity, a soothing balm for his conscience or a tradition to be followed. Man's inability to live God's words, makes a mockery of them. How many Christians follow Christ's teaching to 'turn the other cheek' or 'to love thy neighbour as thyself'? How many Muslims follow Mohammed's precept to 'hold God above everything else'? How many Hindus 'bear the torch of righteousness at all cost'? How many Buddhists live the 'life of pure compassion' expounded by Buddha? How many Zoroastrians 'think truly, speak truly, act truly'? God's Truth cannot be ignored. Because men do ignore It a tremendous adverse reaction is produced, and the world finds itself in a cauldron of suffering through hate, conflicting ideologies and war, and nature's rebellion in the form of floods, famines, earthquakes and other disasters. Ultimately, when the tide of suffering is at its flood, God manifests anew in human form to guide mankind to the destruction of its self-created evil, and re-establish it in the Way of Truth.

My Silence and the imminent breaking of my Silence is to save mankind from the monumental forces of ignorance, and to fulfil the divine Plan of universal unity. The breaking of my Silence will reveal to man the universal Oneness of God, which will bring about the universal brotherhood of man. My Silence had to be. The breaking of my Silence has to be — soon.

# 45

## *Upheaval*

---

When an atom is 'split' an infinite amount of energy is released. Similarly, when my Silence is broken and I utter the WORD infinite wisdom will be released.

When an atom bomb strikes the earth it causes vast devastation. Similarly, when the Word I utter strikes the universe there will be a great material destruction; but there will also take place a tremendous spiritual upheaval.

## 46

## *The Remembered and Forgotten One*

---

I was Rama, I was Krishna, I was this One, I was that One, and now I am Meher Baba. In this form of flesh and blood I am that same Ancient One who alone is eternally worshipped and ignored, ever remembered and forgotten.

\* \* \*

I am that Ancient One whose past is worshipped and remembered, whose present is ignored and forgotten and whose future (Advent) is anticipated with great fervour and longing.

## 47

## *The Question and its Answer*

There is only one question. And once you know the answer to that question there are no more to ask. That one question is the Original Question. And to that Original Question there is only one Final Answer. But between that Question and its Answer there are innumerable false answers.

Out of the depths of unbroken Infinity arose the Question, Who am I? and to that Question there is only one Answer — I am God!

God is Infinite; and His shadow, too, is infinite. Reality is Infinite in its Oneness; Illusion is infinite in its manyness. The one Question arising from the Oneness of the Infinite wanders through an infinite maze of answers which are distorted echoes of Itself resounding from the hollow forms of infinite nothingness.

There is only one Original Question and one Original Answer to it. Between the Original Question and the Original Answer there are innumerable false answers.

These false answers — such as, I am stone, I am bird, I am animal, I am man, I am woman, I am great, I am small — are, in turn, received, tested and discarded until the Question arrives at the right and Final Answer, I AM GOD.

# 48

## *Percentages*

---

*Anna-bhumika*     = God 100% : Divinity 1% =
                     Inclination towards the Self.

*Prana-bhumika*    = God 100% : Divinity 25% =
                     Inspiration about the Self.

*Mana-bhumika*     = God 100% : Divinity 50% =
                     Illumination through the Self.

*Vidnyana-bhumika* = God 100% : Divinity 100% =
                     Realization of the SELF.

## 49

## *Infinite Atmas in Paramatma*

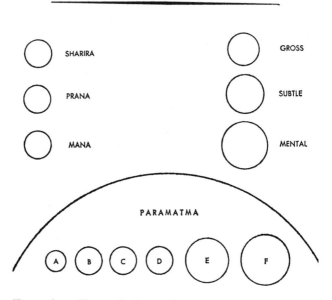

From A to F are all Atmas in Paramatma.

A is the Atma that is not conscious of Sharira, Prana
and Mana, nor of itself (ATMA), and has not the
experience of Gross, Subtle and Mental worlds, nor
of Paramatma.

B is the Atma that is conscious of Sharira, but not
conscious of Prana and Mana, nor of Atma. Has
experience of the Gross world, but has no experience
of Subtle and Mental worlds, nor of Paramatma.

C is the Atma that is conscious of Prana, but not conscious of Sharira and Mana, nor of Atma. Has experience of the Subtle world, but has no experience of Gross and Mental worlds, nor of Paramatma.

D is the Atma that is conscious of Mana, but not conscious of Sharira and Prana, nor of Atma. Has experience of the Mental world, but has no experience of Gross and Subtle worlds, nor of Paramatma.

E is the Atma that is not conscious either of Sharira, Prana, or Mana, but is conscious of Atma. Does not experience Gross, Subtle and Mental worlds, but experiences Paramatma.

F is the Atma that is conscious of Sharira, Prana and Mana, and also conscious of Atma. Experiences Gross, Subtle and Mental worlds, and also Paramatma.

A, B, C, D are in Paramatma, but are not conscious of Atma (SELF), and have not the experience of Paramatma.

E and F are likewise in Paramatma, but are conscious of Atma and experience Paramatma.

The E state of Atma is the Goal of Atmas.

So the sum and substance is: A (unconscious of Sharira, Prana and Mana), in order to attain the state of E (also unconscious of Sharira, Prana and Mana) has necessarily to pass through the states of B, C and D (conscious of Sharira, Prana and Mana).

All Atmas are in Paramatma. Paramatma is Infinite.

In the Infinite Paramatma are infinite Atmas. Therefore:

A is eternally infinite.

B is innumerable and comprises the gross manifestation, from a speck of dust to human beings, inclusive.

C comprises a limited number of subtle-conscious Atmas.

D comprises a few — the mental-conscious Atmas.

E comprises fewer still — the God-realized Atmas.

F comprises the Five Qutubs, and Jeevanmuktas and Paramhansas.

# 50

# *The One and The Zero*

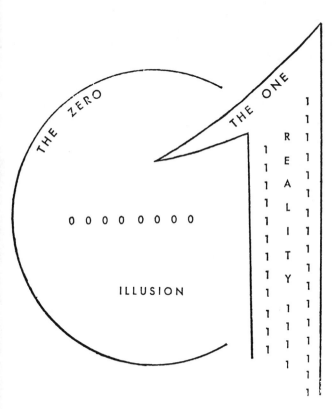

God is generally spoken of as being One. We use the
term One as being opposite to the Many. One we name

REALITY or GOD; Many we name ILLUSION or CREATION.

However, strictly speaking, no number, not even one, can depict ONE who is indivisibly One without a second. Even to call this ONE 'One' is incorrect. We do not speak of the Ocean as One. It just is Ocean. The ONE simply IS.

The ONE is one complete whole and simultaneously a series of ones within the ONE. Illusion is a ZERO and simultaneously a series of zeros within the ZERO. These zeros have no value, except a false value according to their position in relation to the ONE. In actual fact the zeros have no existence — their existence is mere appearance in Illusion, the big ZERO.

# 51

## *The One Original Real Nothing*

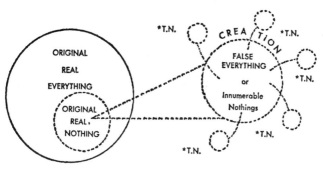

*Temporary Nothings

The Original real EVERYTHING is Infinite and Eternal. Being everything it accommodates within itself the Original Real NOTHING. NOTHING is the shadow of EVERYTHING.

The Substance (EVERYTHING) being Infinite and Eternal, its shadow must also be infinite and eternal. At times the shadow appears to be small and at times to stretch into huge shapes. But even when it seems to have disappeared, it is still within the Substance latently.

Out of the NOTHING contained within the EVERYTHING is projected infinite and eternal Nothingness — the Creation, or False Everything.

The Original Real EVERYTHING is One, Infinite and Eternal. The Original Real NOTHING, being in the Real

EVERYTHING is also one, infinite and eternal. But the False Everything that is projected from the Real NOTHING comprising innumerable nothings or all things in Creation, is innately and unendingly dual.

Within these nothings are innumerable temporary nothings such as, What is the matter with you? Nothing. What did you eat? Nothing. What is in your hand? Nothing. What do you see? Nothing. And so there is no end to the action and reaction of the experience of Nothingness by the innumerable nothings of False Everything which are projected from the One Original Real NOTHING which is infinite.

The Original Real EVERYTHING is Infinite and Eternal; in it is the Original Real NOTHING. Innumerable nothings manifest out of the One Original Real Nothing. And from these nothings is a continuous flow of temporary nothings. And so there are nothings and the no-things of nothing within the One Original Real NOTHING. When you compare these nothings with the One Original Real NOTHING they are indeed *nothing*.

NOTHING is in EVERYTHING; EVERYTHING would not be a complete whole without NOTHING.

The NOTHING that is in EVERYTHING gives birth to nothing that seems everything. Because NOTHING is, everything seems to be.

All activity everywhere in creation is but a play of everything and nothing. When there is a complete cessation of this activity the NOTHING prevails. When this NOTHING is attained you have EVERYTHING. Relatively, therefore, the NOTHING is EVERYTHING, whereas that which we call everything is nothing.

# 52

## *The Procession of Creation*

---

God is Infinite and Eternal. And His Imagination is also Infinite and Eternal. God's Imagination is unending, and the Creation which is the product of His Imagination goes on endlessly expanding. How can man imagine this Imagination with his finite imagining? His highest flights of imagination (intellect) can never bring him the faintest idea of God's Imagination. And God's Reality is beyond this again. When you cannot imagine even the Imagination of God, how infinitely more impossible it is to fathom His Reality.

In what is called space numberless universes are continuously created, sustained and destroyed. This procession of creation continues so long as God goes on imagining. And when God's Imagination is suspended, as it is at moments in Eternity when God withdraws Himself into His Sound Sleep State (just as a man's imagination ceases when he is in deep sleep), the Creation is withdrawn and dissolved (Mahapralaya).

Creation, Preservation and Dissolution are based on Ignorance. In fact there is no such thing as *creation*, so *preservation* and *dissolution* never actually occur. The very cosmos has no foundation save that of Ignorance.

Ignorance believes: The cosmos is a reality; birth, death, old age, wealth, honour, are real.

Knowledge knows: The cosmos is a dream. God alone is Real.

# 53

## *The Dream of Materialism*

The condition of the world, the strife and uncertainty that is everywhere, the general dissatisfaction with and rebellion against any and every situation shows that the ideal of material perfection is an empty dream and proves the existence of an eternal Reality beyond materiality; for if this Reality did not exist, the increased material well-being of millions of people which science has brought about would have produced contentment and satisfaction, and the tremendous imagination science has projected into the general consciousness would have let loose happiness. Man thinks that there was never so much achievement and promise of greater achievement as now; but the fact is there was never such wide-spread distrust and dissatisfaction and misery. The promises of science have been proved empty, and its vision false.

Reality alone is real; the only *true* thing that can be said is, Reality exists and all that is not the Real has no existence except as illusion. In their heart of hearts people know this and, although for a time, they get beguiled by the false promises of illusion and think of them as real, nothing else than the Real can satisfy them, and they become fed up with the misery that the almost limitless play of false imagination gradually brings about. This is the condition of the general people now. Even I am fed up and miserable. Why should I be so, when I am free? Because as the Buddha said, 'I am eternally free and eternally bound.'

[ 88 ]

I am bound because of people's bondage, and fed up and miserable because of their fed-upness and misery. The greatest scientists themselves are becoming dismayed at the areas of knowledge still beyond them and appalled at what their discoveries may unleash. It will not be long now before they admit complete bafflement and affirm the existence of this eternal Reality which men call God, and which is unapproachable through the intellect.

The ordinary man, although he is completely fed up with being cheated of the prize that materialism promises and appears to deny the existence of God and to have lost faith in everything but the immediate advantage, never really loses his inborn belief in God and faith in the Reality which is beyond the illusion of the moment. His apparent doubt and loss of faith is because of a desperation of mind only, it does not touch his heart. Look at Peter. He denied Christ. Desperation made his mind deny, but in his heart he knew that Christ was what He was. The ordinary man never loses faith. He is as one who climbs up a mountain a certain distance and, experiencing cold and difficulty of breathing, returns to the foot of the mountain. But the scientific mind goes on up the mountain until its heart freezes and dies. But this mind is becoming so staggered by the vastness still beyond it, that it will be forced to admit the hopelessness of its quest and turn to God, the Reality.

# 54

## *The Now*

---

Astronomers speak of time in terms of billions, trillions and aeons of years. Even these figures are not adequate for their mathematical calculations and they may be required to coin new terms.

If I were to try and explain in astronomical terms the beginning and end of time, it would never depict the beginning and end of time in Eternity.

There is always an 'ago' and there is always an 'after' to every point in time. The 'yesterdays' of the past and the 'tomorrows' of the future hinge on a point in time which is the NOW of the present moment in Eternity.

In a flight of imagination imagining the beginning and the end of the NOW of the present moment in Eternity, one can at the most either add or subtract a measure of time; but this would be nothing more than an adding or erasing of zeros. No amount of swing, even of aeons of cycles, in the sweep of time can give an iota of concept of any beginning or end of the NOW in Eternity.

# 55

## *Is*

In Reality there is only One. In Illusion there are many. The reason why there is so much confusion as to whether there is one God or many is because God is so Infinitely One.

Even to say, There is one God is wrong. God is so infinitely One that He cannot even be called One. One may only say, One *is*. The word 'God' is only an attempt to give that One a name, for in actuality He has no name. Even to say that God is One implies the possibility of two. For one to say there are many Gods is madness.

God is that 'One' playing innumerable roles. For example, one of you is sitting with his eyes closed and in his imagination he creates innumerable things, and in the very act of imagining them he preserves them. Then he opens his eyes, and in so doing destroys all the things his imagination had created and held together. Thus the same person played different roles, that of creator, sustainer and dissolver.

Again, another is in sound sleep — which is the Original State of God — people say he is asleep; but in sound sleep he is not even conscious of himself as himself. When he wakes up people say, he is awake, and when he brushes his teeth, people say, he is brushing his teeth. And when he is seen walking, running about, speaking, singing, etc., he is merely playing different roles. He cannot be more than one, for he is only one.

All that we can ever say is: God is, or, One is.

There are two things that exist: One and Many. One we call God; Many we call Illusion. Why? Because in Reality only One *is*. Even to call this One, One, is not right — One *is*.

# 56

## *Infinite Individuality Asserts Indivisible Oneness*

There is no scope for separateness in the vastness of the Infinite Ocean of Indivisible Oneness. How then can there be any room for individuality in indivisibility? In the indivisible unlimited Ocean of Reality, how can there be scope for each drop that has fully awakened to Reality to individually proclaim: I am the Ocean!

The moment the drop has been stirred to consciousness, it isolates itself into a separate entity and acquires an individuality, a false I-AM-ness. This awakened 'I' is enveloped in falseness that grows with every step of its increased consciousness in proportion to its field of impressions and expression. This falseness that at first helps the drop to establish individuality in the indivisible Ocean, becomes the perpetual hindrance that keeps the drop from knowing itself as the Ocean. The 'I' has to get rid of the falseness before it can realize Who it is in reality.

At the end of the journey, when at long last the Goal is reached by the grace of the Perfect Master, this falseness is entirely removed and the 'I' alone remains with its supreme Self-knowledge — saying, My falseness is gone — I am God!

Thus, when each individual drop sheds its false awareness of being other than the Ocean, it proclaims itself as the Infinite Indivisible Ocean. At the instant its falseness, its very own falseness is removed, the drop asserts its Infinite Individuality. It then consciously and continuously experiences itself for all time as being without a second: the Almighty, Infinite and indivisible Paramatma. This is the I-am-God state. This is how every Atma, from the instant its consciousness is unburdened of falseness (i.e., impressions) for all time, asserts itself as the Paramatma, God Absolute.

# 57

## *Three Conditions*

---

God experiences three conditions of consciousness:
(1) His Original State; (2) Helplessness; (3) All-
powerfulness.

### *The Original State*

In this state God, unconscious of His Infinite Power,
Bliss and Existence, is perfectly at peace. This state
can well be compared with the sound sleep state of a
person.

### *Helplessness*

In this state God is also unconscious of His being
Infinite, and experiences helplessness in human form.
He is constantly worried about something. He finds no
peace. Owing to innumerable anxieties and problems,
He tries all the time to seek His original state. To do
this He induces forgetfulness through intoxications. He
wants to forget everything. In His state of helplessness,
His first experience of forgetfulness has so great an
effect on Him that He desires above all to return again
to the oblivion that He has experienced. He tries to
regain this state through sleep. Thus sleep becomes a
dire necessity.

But since in sleep He is unconscious, He is not able
to bring His experience of forgetfulness back into His
waking state; and so He finds no solution to His
helplessness.

## All-powerfulness

His helplessness increases day by day. When it becomes unlimited it ends in the state of All-powerfulness. In this state God consciously forgets ever having had a limited individuality and knows Himself as Infinite Existence, Bliss and All-powerfulness.

# 58

## *Truth is of God, Law is of Illusion*

There are two things: Truth and Law.
Truth belongs to God, Law belongs to Illusion.

Illusion is infinitely vast yet it is governed by Law.
The 'law of cause and effect', which none can escape,
belongs to this Law.

Law is bondage. Truth is Freedom.
Law upholds Ignorance. Truth upholds Reality.
Law governs imagination which binds you to
  Illusion.
Truth sets you free from Illusion.

Although it is the nature of imagination to run riot,
it is restricted to the definite and minutely precise
pattern of bindings created and upheld by the law of
bondage.

The moment imagining ceases, the shackles of the
Law are broken and Freedom is experienced in the
realization of the Truth.

It is impossible for one of oneself to overcome the
operation of the Law and merge in the Truth. Only
those who are one with God can take you beyond the
bounds of the Law and give you the experience of the
Freedom — which is the Truth.

# 59

## *Shadows of Knowledge, Power, Bliss*

---

God has three Infinite aspects: Knowledge, Power, Bliss. It is from these that man derives his three finite aspects of mind, energy, matter.

The three aspects of God are interlinked; Bliss depends on Power and Power depends on Knowledge. Similarly, the three aspects of man are interlinked; matter depends on energy and energy depends on mind.

As a human being you are one homogeneous entity of these three finite aspects (mind-energy-matter), which are but the *shadows* of the three Infinite aspects of God (Knowledge-Power-Bliss).

# 60

## *The World is a Prison*

---

The world is a prison in which the Soul experiences being behind the bars of its gross-subtle-mental body — the Soul, eternally free, lone Sovereign and supreme Lord! Illusion's hold is so strong that the Soul experiences itself as serf rather than Soul.

Illusion stages the Lord's imprisonment so perfectly and establishes His serfdom so convincingly that even at the moment when the Perfect Master bestows His Grace on the Soul it experiences itself as breaking out through the bars of a prison which never existed.

The Soul's apparent imprisonment becomes so suffocatingly unbearable that it — by the Master's Grace — literally tears itself free; and the feeling of exultation is as powerful as was its feeling of suffocation. The experience of both imprisonment and release is of Illusion; but the experience of the final Freedom is of Reality. The emancipated Soul then experiences continuously and eternally its own infinite freedom.

The world exists only as long as the Soul experiences bondage; when the Soul realizes itself as Reality the world vanishes — for it never was. And the Soul experiences itself as being Infinite and Eternal.

# 61

## *Purposelessness in Infinite Existence*

---

Reality is Existence infinite and eternal.

Existence has no purpose by virtue of its being real, infinite and eternal.

Existence exists. Being Existence it *has to* exist. Hence Existence, the Reality, cannot have any purpose. It just is. It is self-existing.

Everything — the things and the beings — *in* Existence has a purpose. All things and beings have a purpose and must have a purpose, or else they cannot *be* in existence as what they are. Their very being in existence proves their purpose; and their *sole purpose* in existing is to become shed of purpose, i.e., to become purposeless.

Purposelessness is of Reality; to have a purpose is to be lost in falseness.

Everything exists only because it has a purpose. The moment that purpose has been accomplished, everything disappears and Existence is manifested as self-existing Self.

Purpose presumes a direction and since Existence, being everything and everywhere, cannot have any direction, directions must always be in nothing and lead nowhere.

Hence to have a purpose is to create a false goal.

Love alone is devoid of all purpose and a spark of Divine Love sets fire to all purposes.

The Goal of Life in Creation is to arrive at purposelessness, which is the state of Reality.

# 62

## *Mental Consciousness*

Those on the Mental planes are not conscious of the Gross or Subtle planes. How then is it possible for one on the Mental plane to speak, eat, drink, etc.—in short, to perform actions the same as those of an ordinary man on the Gross plane?

It is just as we hear of people walking or eating, drinking, writing, pilfering and so on in their sleep, and yet they are absolutely unconscious of doing these gross actions. It is not uncommon for a person to talk in his sleep. All those around him can hear him speaking in his sleep, but the person himself is not aware or conscious of his own speaking. In the same way, the ones on the Mental planes are totally unconscious of gross and subtle actions and spheres, although all their gross and subtle actions are the outcome of their thoughts and feelings — the functions of Mind.

Those on the Mental planes, while controlling the thoughts and consequent actions of others on the Subtle and Gross planes, are themselves not conscious of their own gross and subtle actions. This is because such a thing as gross or subtle does not exist for them. Their consciousness is totally severed and dissociated from the Gross and Subtle spheres. For instance, an ordinary man cannot but say he is man, for he identifies himself with the gross body. He is gross-conscious and his consciousness of being is associated directly only with the gross body (sharira). Another, who is on the Subtle planes, cannot but identify himself with the subtle body (prana); while yet another, who is on the Mental planes cannot but identify himself with the mental body (mana). This 'Mind personified' atma of the Mental plane, who as MANA cannot by any remotest possibility ever identify itself as Sharira or Prana, is wholly dissociated from the gross and subtle bodies and cannot experience the Gross and Subtle spheres.

For example, let us imagine India as representing the Gross world, England as the Subtle world, and America as the Mental world. If A is in India he has full consciousness of India and has totally NO consciousness of England and America. When A goes to England, he is obviously neither in India nor in America. He is now entirely removed from these two places. He possesses full consciousness as before, but this same full consciousness is now absolutely and entirely in England. India is totally dropped from the orbit of his consciousness, while America has not yet entered into it.

Similarly, when A goes to America, he is neither in India nor in England. He is now entirely withdrawn from these two places. He continues to possess full consciousness as before but this same full consciousness is now absolutely and entirely in America. India and England are totally dropped from the orbit of his consciousness.

Again, consciousness may be compared to the light from a flashlight or torch. The area illuminated by the light of the torch represents the particular plane of consciousness. Imagine three regions stationed at increasing distance from you termed M, S and G, to represent the Mental, Subtle and Gross planes; these are in complete darkness to begin with.

When the light of the torch is directed on G (representing the Gross plane), which is furthest from yourself, this region comes under the direct focus of light and is fully lit, with its immediate vicinity dimly glowing from the reflection of that focussed light. The areas S and M are yet in total darkness.

If this light is at last made to shift nearer toward you to focus on S (representing the Subtle plane), the region G is left in total darkness. Now S alone is fully illuminated, with the dim glow of reflection having moved to the vicinity of the newly focussed area of light.

If this focus of light is shifted still nearer toward you to M (representing the Mental plane), both the regions G and S are left in total darkness. It is now M that receives the full and direct focus of light, and it alone is fully illuminated; while the dim glow of reflection is automatically thrown around this newly focussed area of light.

When the focus of this same light is finally shifted still nearer, not only toward you but actually ON you, it is yourself that is fully lit, and all the three regions, G, S and M, are in total darkness. You are thus fully conscious only of your SELF. This final focussing of the light (consciousness) on to your Self is the Goal. This is Self-illumination, or in other words God-realization.

Any action performed by one on the Mental planes, as observed by the gross-conscious or subtle-conscious atmas, is nothing but a gross or subtle manifestation of a mental action. The apparently gross action that you on the Gross plane see performed by one on the Mental plane, is merely the pattern of that mental function translated on the screen of your own gross consciousness. Hence, the one on the Mental plane, totally dissociated from the gross and subtle, does NOT speak, eat, or drink in the sense that those on the Gross plane eat, drink and speak, though he appears to do so. When you see such a one eating, drinking, speaking, etc., it is nothing but your own gross interpretation of the reflection of his mental activity.

For example, when you see the moon reflected in a lake, to all intents and purposes it is in the water as long as your gaze is directed at the lake.

The moon is not in the water. The reflection of the moon is in the water; but it appears as if the moon is in the water.

So, the consciousness of the one on the Mental planes is not here. The reflection of his consciousness is here; but it appears as if he was conscious of the Gross plane.

When one on the Mental planes performs an action, that act cannot be comprehended by any one having consciousness only of the subtle or the gross. That same act is interpreted differently by the ones on the Subtle planes and the ones on the Gross plane, in the light of their own respective consciousnesses.

In short, the function of Mind of one on the Mental planes, when received by you on the Gross plane, comes through the channel of your gross consciousness and reaches you in the shape or movement familiar to your range of awareness and capacity of comprehension.

# 63

## *The Working of the Avatar*

---

The Avatar draws upon Himself the universal suffering, but He is sustained under the stupendous burden by His infinite Bliss and His infinite sense of humour. The Avatar is the Axis or Pivot of the universe, the Pin of the grinding-stones of evolution, and so has a responsibility towards everyone and everything.

At each moment in time He is able to fulfil singly and together the innumerable aspects of His universal duty because His actions are in no way constrained by time and distance and the here and now of the senses. While engaged in any particular action on the gross plane He is simultaneously working on all the inner planes. Unlike the actions of ordinary men, the Avatar's every action on the gross plane brings about numberless and far-reaching results on the different planes of consciousness. His working on the inner planes is effortless and continues of itself, but because of the very nature of grossness His work on the gross plane entails great exertion.

As a rule each action of an ordinary person is motivated by a solitary aim serving a solitary purpose; it can hit only one target at a time and bring about one specific result. But with the Avatar, He being the Centre of each one, any single action of His on the gross plane brings about a network of diverse results for people and objects everywhere.

The Avatar's action on the gross plane is like the throwing of a main switch in an electric power-house, which immediately and simultaneously releases an immense force through many circuits, putting into action various branches of service such as factories and fans, trains and trolleys and lighting for cities and villages.

An ordinary physical action of the Avatar releases immense forces in the inner planes and so becomes the starting point for a chain of working, the repercussions and overtones of which are manifest at all levels and are universal in range and effect.

Everything in the universe is, and from the beginning has been, a materialization of the divine Original Whim working out irrevocably without default, deflection or defeat. It is the unfolding upon the screen of consciousness of the film of creation, sequence after sequence, according to the pattern that issued from the Original Whim. However, when God as God-Man plays the role of Audience He can alter or erase at His avataric whim any thing or happening which was destined from the Original Whim. But the very arising of the avataric whim was inherent in the Original Whim.

The Sufis distinguish between Qaza or destined occurrences, and Qadar or happenings which are impulsive or 'accidental'. The Avatar's or Qutub's actions are impulsive and arise from their infinite compassion; and the functioning of this whim relieves and gives beauty and charm to what would otherwise be a rigid determinism.

The Qutub's actions bring about modifications in the previously determined divine Plan, but they are limited in extent. But the Avatar's interventions bring about modifications on a universal scale. For instance, supposing that it was divinely ordained for a war to occur in 1950. It must take place at the appointed time, and the train of events which follows will punctually meet the present time-table. However, if the Avatar is in the world at the time He might, in His exercise of Qadar, ward off the catastrophe by some particular action on the gross plane. And so in the relentless working out of the laws of Nature there can enter the inexplicable divine caprice, spelling out peace instead of war in the diary of man. Kabir has said:

Kabir rekha karam kee kabhee na meete Ram
Meetanhar samarth hai para samajh kiya hai kam.

O Kabir! The lines of fate are never effaced by Rama; He is All-powerful and can undo destiny, but He never does so for He has given full thought to what He has planned.

The Avatar does not as a rule interfere with the working out of human destinies. He will do so only in times of grave necessity—when He deems it absolutely necessary from His all-encompassing point of view. For a single alteration in the planned and imprinted pattern in which each line and dot is interdependent, means a shaking up and a re-linking of an unending chain of possibilities and events. The least divergence from the pre-drawn line of Fate not only requires infinite adjustments within the immediate orbit of the individual concerned, but involves in its interminable repercussions all those connected by the bond of past sanskaras.

The avataric whim is also part of the divine Destiny. Qaza provides for the absolute necessity of the Avatar's 'chance' intervention, and the very unpredictability of this intervention is predicted in Qaza — for His infinite compassion, because of which His intervention occurs, may not be denied.

In the working out of the avataric whim there is not the least element of chance. The aim of the whim's action is perfect and its result is precise.

An ordinary person's whim, when expressed, may

have consequences quite outside itself, as illustrated by the following story. A drunken man was passing by a wood-apple tree and had a whim to taste one of its fruits. As a rule a drunkard has a distaste for sour or tart things because they nullify the effects of drink, so this man's wanting a wood-apple was purely a whim, independent of thought or real desire. He picked up a stone and threw it at the tree. The stone missed any of the apples, killed a bird, scared away many others and fell on the head of a traveller resting beneath the tree. Thus the haphazard expression of the drunkard's whim not only failed to accomplish the whim but brought about results completely outside it. The whim was merely an unrelated fancy, and the action stemming from it had no connection with its object.

This sort of thing can never happen in the exercise of the Avatar's whim. Arising from compassion and expression of Perfection it is perfect in its aim and results.

# 64

## *Forgive and Forget*

People ask God for forgiveness. But since God is everything and everyone, who is there for Him to forgive? Forgiveness of the created was already there in His act of creation. But still people ask God's forgiveness, and He forgives them. But they, instead of forgetting that for which they asked forgiveness, forget that God has forgiven them, and, instead, remember the things they were forgiven — and so nourish the seed of wrongdoing, and it bears its fruit again. Again and again they plead for forgiveness, and again and again the Master says, I forgive.

But it is impossible for men to forget their wrongdoings and the wrongs done to them by others. And since they cannot forget, they find it hard to forgive. But forgiveness is the best charity. (It is easy to give the poor money and goods when one has plenty, but to forgive is hard; but it is the best thing if one can do it.)

Instead of men trying to forgive one another they fight. Once they fought with their hands and with clubs. Then with spears and bows and arrows. Then with guns and cannon. Then they invented bombs and carriers for them. Now they have developed missiles that can destroy millions of other men thousands of miles away, and they are prepared to use them. The weapons used change, but the aggressive pattern of man remains the same.

Now men are planning to go to the moon. And the first to get there will plant his nation's flag on it, and that nation will say, It is mine. But another nation will dispute the claim and they will fight here on this earth for possession of that moon. And whoever goes there, what will he find? Nothing but himself. And if people go on to Venus they will still find nothing but themselves. Whether men soar to outer space or dive to the bottom of the deepest ocean they will find themselves as they are, unchanged, because they will not have forgotten themselves nor remembered to exercise the charity of forgiveness.

Supremacy over others will never cause a man to find a change in himself; the greater his conquests the stronger is his confirmation of what his mind tells him — that there is no God other than his own power. And he remains separated from God, the Absolute Power.

But when the same mind tells him that there is *something* which may be called God, and, further, when it prompts him to search for God that he may see Him face to face, he begins to forget himself and to forgive others for whatever he has suffered from them.

And when he has forgiven everyone and has completely forgotten himself, he finds that God has forgiven him everything, and he remembers Who, in reality, he is.

# 65

## *Ignorance Personified*

---

God is Indivisible One, and is indivisibly in each one and everything.

What is it then that causes apparent divisions? There are no divisions as such, but there is an appearance of separateness because of ignorance. This means that everything is of ignorance and that every one is Ignorance personified.

A drop in an ocean is not separate from the ocean. It is a bubble over the drop that gives it an appearance of separateness, but when the bubble bursts the drop is not, and the indivisible ocean is.

When the bubble of ignorance bursts the self realizes its oneness with the indivisible Self.

Words that proceed from the Source of Truth have real meaning. But when men speak these words as their own, the words become meaningless.

# Bibliography

---

## Books by Meher Baba

*Beams from Meher Baba on the Spiritual Panorama.* Walnut Creek, CA: Sufism Reoriented, 1958.

*Discourses.* 7th revised edition. Myrtle Beach, SC: Sheriar Press, 1987.

*God Speaks.* 2nd edition. New York: Dodd, Mead, 1973.

*God to Man and Man to God: the Discourses of Meher Baba.* Myrtle Beach, SC: Sheriar Press, 1984.

*Life At Its Best.* New York: Harper & Row, 1972.

## Selected List of Books about Meher Baba

*The Beloved* by Naosherwan Anzar. Myrtle Beach, SC: Sheriar Press, 1974.

*The Dance of Love* by Margaret Craske. Myrtle Beach, SC: Sheriar Press, 1980.

*The God-Man* by Charles B. Purdom. Myrtle Beach, SC: Sheriar Press, 1971.

*Love Alone Prevails* by Kitty Davy. Myrtle Beach, SC: Sheriar Press, 1981.

There are many books by and about Meher Baba. For a free booklist or further information contact: Sheriar Press, 3005 Highway 17 North ByPass, Myrtle Beach, SC 29577, U.S.A.

# *Biographical*

Merwan S. Irani, named Meher Baba ("The Compassionate One") by His early disciples, was born in 1894 in Poona, India. Between the years of 1913 and 1921, the five Perfect Masters, or *Sadgurus,* of that time led Him to realize His identity and universal mission as the *Avatar of the Age* — the God-Man, the Buddha, the Christ. After working intensively with an intimate group of disciples for some years, Baba began to observe silence in 1925, and throughout the more than four decades of His spiritual activities on Earth, He did not utter a word. From His work in India and the East with the mad, infirm, and poor and with spiritually advanced souls to His contact with thousands of people in the West, Meher Baba has awakened innumerable persons to the quest for higher consciousness and their own ultimate reality.

Throughout the years, Meher Baba indicated that the breaking of His Silence would come in a way and at a time that no one could imagine, and that His "speaking the Word" after the appearance of utter defeat would be His only real miracle in this incarnation as God in human form: "When I break My Silence, the impact will jolt the world out of its spiritual lethargy . . . What will happen when I break My Silence is what has never happened before . . . The breaking of My Silence will reveal to man the universal Oneness of God, which will bring about the universal brotherhood of man."

Declaring that His work had been completed 100% to His satisfaction and that the results of that work would soon begin to manifest, Meher Baba dropped his body on January 31st, 1969.